RL 7.9

EARTH'S HIDDEN TREASURES

EARTH'S HIDDEN TREASURES

SANDRA DOWNS

TWENTY-FIRST CENTURY BOOKS
BROOKFIELD, CONNECTICUT

FOR SUE—A GEM OF A SISTER

Library of Congress Cataloging-in-Publication Data
Downs, Sandra Friend.
Earth's hidden treasures / Sandra Downs.
p. cm. — (Exploring planet earth)
Includes bibliographical references and index.
Summary: Explains what rocks, minerals, and gemstones
are found on the earth and how they are used by people.
ISBN 0-7613-1411-3 (lib. bdg.)
1. Minerals—Juvenile literature. 2. Rocks—Juvenile literature.
[1. Rocks. 2. Minerals.] I. Title. II. Series.
QE365.2.D68 1999
549—dc21 98-48502 CIP AC

Published by Twenty-First Century Books
A Division of The Millbrook Press, Inc.
2 Old New Milford Road
Brookfield, Connecticut 06804
Visit us at our Web site: www.millbrookpress.com

Cover photograph courtesy of Photo Researchers, Inc. (© Jacana)

Photographs courtesy of The National Audubon Society Collection/Photo Researchers: pp. 11
(© Soames Summerhays), 12 (© Mary M. Thacher), 14 (bottom © John R. Foster), 15 (©
Charles D. Winters), 18 (top © Charles D. Winters; bottom © M. Claye/Jacana);, 19 (top right
© Joyce Photographics; bottom © Vaughan Fleming/SPL), 23 (© Biophoto Associates), 35 (©
1997 Stephen L. Saks), 36 (left © E. R. Degginger), 42 (center © Charles D. Winters; bottom
© Joyce Photo); © Joel E. Arem: pp. 13, 14 (top), 19 (top left), 21, 26, 27, 38, 42 (top); © GIA:
p. 25; © Sandra Downs: pp. 29, 44 © 1998 Jeff Scovil: pp. 33, 36 (right), 49; Peter Arnold,
Inc.: p. 39 (© Chlaus Lotscher); Scala/Art Resource, NY: p. 51

CONTENTS

TREASURES WE TAKE FOR GRANTED

TASSOS KNELT, EXAMINING THE DARK BLUE CLAY. As waves lapped at his feet, he plunged his fingers into the thick, sticky mass. He dropped fistfuls into his basket. The clay left a quick-drying cast on his hands, which he wiped onto his shirt. He hefted the basket and sank into the ooze as he walked back to the village, and his kiln. He would make many jars this day.

JONATHAN CLENCHED HIS MUSKET TIGHTLY. Philadelphia must stay free, at any cost. Food was scarce. Lead, used for musket balls, was even scarcer. Citizens melted precious clock weights, curtain weights, and pewter for the war effort. Yesterday his brother, Nathaniel, responded to General Roberdeau's plea for stout-hearted men to join him on the Pennsylvania frontier, men who would brave great dangers to dig and smelt lead desperately needed by the Continental Army. Jonathan reached into his pocket and fingered his handful of musket balls. Would the new supply of lead reach the army in time?

CAREFULLY FOLLOWING THE DIRECTIONS IN HIS HANDBOOK, Roger connected the last wire to his crystal set. A slight crackle grew into a recognizable sound, the sound of music. Roger ran into the parlor. "Dad! My radio's working!"

An ancient potter . . . a Revolutionary War soldier . . . a young Boy Scout . . . What do they have in common? They depend on minerals. Minerals are the building blocks of rocks, and contain essential elements needed for life. Minerals are such a part of our lives that they surround us constantly: in the machines we use, in the walls of our homes, in even the simplest of tools. They're used in every conveyance, from bicycles and automobiles to airplanes and spaceships. Our computers—including the electricity that flows through the wires to feed them, and the streams of information that pass through them—all depend on minerals. Everything we touch, everything we do, is in some way influenced by the geologic bounty of our planet.

We think of rocks as ancient, of minerals as growing over centuries, but geology is a dynamic phenomenon. New minerals form every day, born from magma flowing deep beneath the earth's surface. Old minerals become new, as weathering changes their chemical compositions or heat and pressure trigger changes at the atomic level. Rotting logs, fallen leaves, and the bones of mammals settle and compress to become organic minerals: peat, coal, and oil. The genesis of minerals is a history of recycling, as the components from the beginnings of the earth still exist in the rocks and minerals of today.

THE EARTH GIVES BIRTH

1

As Earth formed, cascades of magma poured forth to form burning seas. The magma cooled and grew hard, creating vast regions of igneous rock.

Igneous rocks formed below the earth's surface are intrusive, while those formed by lava flows on the surface are extrusive. Vast stretches of basalt make up the ocean floors. Giant batholiths, pools of magma that solidified in place, contain some of the world's richest mineral deposits and the world's largest crystals. Besides basalt, other common igneous rocks are diabase, granite, and gabbro.

Liquid rock. A lava flow at the Kilauea Rift, Hawaii. As the lava cools, new rock is formed.

Waves beat steadily against shorelines, eroding the new rocks. The formation of mountains uplifted and shifted great slabs of rock. Deep below the earth's surface, magma continued to push upward. The violent reaction from the heat of fresh magma touch-

Gneiss, isn't it? You can see garnets at lower right in this gneissic rock.

ing existing rocks created new and different rocks. Pressure from mountain building and heat from magma forced atomic-level changes to the igneous deposits, generating metamorphic rock.

Metamorphic rocks show signs of being crushed by great forces. Gneiss displays its crystals in striped bands. Schist rolls in wavy folds. Marble has colorful banding. The mica crystals embedded in slate all lie in the same direction.

Life appeared in the oceans: one-celled amoebas, then larger creatures including corals and crustaceans. Their remains settled to the ocean floor, building thick sediment. Ocean floors lifted during more mountain building, creating dry land. The compressed remains of sea creatures, as well as the solidified mud and silts, became sedimentary rock.

Sedimentary rocks are the youngest rocks, formed by deposition of minerals and organic materials carried away through ero-

MAGMA: MINERAL STEW

All the components for minerals exist in magma, the liquid stew of elements that bubbles below the surface of the earth, melting and recycling rocks. As magma rises towards the earth's surface, it creates pipes of molten rock. Minerals coat the sides of the magma pipe as the magma cools. Each mineral has a specific temperature at which it forms. Layers upon layers of different minerals can crystallize on top of each other. When magma cools slowly, giant crystals form. One mine in Russia is entirely inside a single feldspar crystal.

When magma cools quickly, dense rocks and minerals form. Pyrite (also known as fool's gold) is a dense iron mineral that forms this way.

When magma cools instantly, glassy rocks, such as obsidian, form.

INSTANT ROCKS

Obsidian is highly prized by primitive cultures. This natural glass was chipped into razor-sharp points for knives, spears, and arrowheads.

Obsidian isn't the only rock that develops instantly. When lightning strikes sand, it burrows into the ground, fusing the sand into a glass tube to create a fulgurite. These rocks always have a smooth, glassy interior and a rough, sandy exterior. If the lightning skimmed the surface of the sand, the fulgurite may have multiple branches, like coral. The largest fulgurite ever found was 5 feet (1.5 meters) long.

Humans create instant rocks as well. We melt sand into glass on purpose, and sometimes by accident. To melt sand requires a temperature of 2,400° F (1316° C). The process of smelting ore involves melting rock to pour off the important metallic minerals. Before high-temperature molds were invented, molten metal was poured into a shape sculpted in sand. The sand would melt into a useless glass, something you can find if you visit an old iron furnace site.

This obsidian would make lots of cutting and scraping tools, as well as points, or arrowheads like the one shown on page 49.

More recently, instant rocks have been formed by war. The first atomic bomb test, in Trinity, New Mexico, created an artificial sea of glassy green rock. Oil fires in Kuwait during the Persian Gulf War created deep black expanses of glass on the desert plain.

Fulgurite is harder to find than you might expect because it is often very fragile and breaks soon after it's formed.

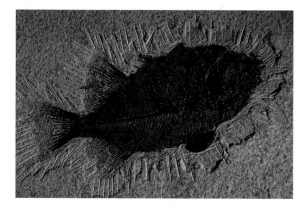

A fossil of phareodus, *an early fish, in sedimentary rock.*

sion and evaporation, disintegration, and decomposition. They form in strata—layers, like blankets—on top of each other. Common sedimentary rocks are sandstone, shale, limestone, and gypsum. Fossils are found only in sedimentary rocks.

Soft, crumbly gypsum is a sedimentary rock you use every day. It's in the wallboard and plaster used on the walls and ceilings of your house and school. It's in your toothpaste, and in some of the ceramics in your bathroom. Gypsum is nontoxic, providing a source of calcium. Baked goods contain gypsum in frosting, baking powder, and self-rising flour, and it's also frequently used to calm an upset stomach.

Glaciers carried away rocks and deposited them far from their origins. After the glaciers receded, rain and snow eroded the freshly uncovered rock. Sedimentary rock turned to metamorphic rock, and metamorphic rock into other metamorphic rock.

Surface water trickled into the earth, carrying loose minerals. Small crevices filled with crystals and ores. Fantastic stalactites and stalagmites grew in caverns. Continued uplifting of the land carried these deposits to mountaintops. Rains weathered the softer rock until the ores and crystals tumbled loose. Heavier pieces settled to the bottom of streambeds. As streams changed course, their precious cargo disappeared under layers of silt and leaves that later turned to deep soil.

This cycle continues in a perpetual dance. Earthquakes tilt and squash solid earth. Magma pours from beneath the Atlantic Ocean as the sea floor spreads; it bursts to life through volcanoes in the "Ring of Fire" around the Pacific Ocean. Rivers spread silt into the sea. The total mass of the earth remains constant: it is the elements, in their constant movement from liquids to solids and back again, that recombine in an endless array of rocks and minerals.

THE ELEMENTS TAKE SHAPE

2

Mica separates easily into thin leaves.

As elements join to create minerals, tiny forces at the atomic level determine exactly what sort of mineral the elements will become. Minerals that are native elements—such as gold, silver, and copper—contain only a single element. Most minerals contain two or more elements.

Just thirteen elements make up 99.5 percent of Earth's solid crust: aluminum, calcium, carbon, oxygen, silicon, iron, sodium, potassium, magnesium, titanium, phosphorus, hydrogen, and manganese. Most minerals contain at least one of these elements.

Based on their elemental composition, minerals can be classified into ten distinct groups. Native elements are one group. Oxides—minerals that contain oxygen plus one or more other elements—are another. Hematite, an iron ore, is a common oxide. Minerals containing carbon are called carbonates. Halides are compounds of chlorine, fluorine, bromine, and iodine. Halite, or rock salt, is one of the halides. There are several other groups that include minerals that contain a certain element. Of these, the most important classification is the silicates, minerals containing silicon. This is the largest group of minerals, containing most of the gemstones and all of the important rock-forming minerals. Almost every rock contains at least one major silicate mineral: quartz, feldspar, or mica. Of over two thousand known kinds of minerals, only fifty or so occur in combinations that create all of Earth's rocks!

Despite the infinite combinations possible, some very different minerals share the same elements. Diamond and graphite are both expressions of the carbon atom. Soft graphite is used in pencils. Diamonds, the hardest mineral on earth, can cut through any substance. Calcite and aragonite are both calcium carbonate. Glittering, icy calcite is hard to the touch. Delicate, feathery aragonite crumbles easily. What makes these minerals so different in nature? Locked in whirling orbits, their atoms form a pattern, the personality of the mineral. The precise alignment of the electrons, set by the heat and pressure under which the mineral developed, defines the mineral's atomic structure—its crystal lattice.

POWERFUL STUFF

When elements combine to form compounds, unusual things can happen. A type of magnet called an alnico magnet contains aluminum, nickel, and cobalt. Nickel is sometimes magnetic, but aluminum and cobalt aren't magnetic at all. Yet, put these three elements together, and they form the strongest magnetic substance in the world!

Other powerful mineral properties caused by combinations of elements include radioactivity, odor, and flavor.

TOUGH!

Atomic structure gives a mineral certain constant characteristics. If you hit a mineral with a hammer, what will happen? The mineral will break, or the hammer might bounce off the mineral, or the hammer might break! Hardness illustrates the relative density of the atoms that make up the mineral. Large atoms, with electrons in loosely arranged orbits, create a soft mineral. A hard mineral has small atoms that are crowded close together.

MOHS SCALE

Mohs Scale of Hardness compares how hard minerals are by how difficult it is to make a scratch on them. The scale starts with the softest mineral, talc. You can scratch talc with your fingernail. Mohs chose topaz to represent hardness level 8. Beryl, a mineral family that includes emerald and aquamarine, is also an 8. The corundum family, at 9, includes sapphires and rubies. The hardest mineral on earth is diamond. Only a diamond can scratch another diamond.

1	TALC
2	GYPSUM
3	CALCITE
4	FLUORITE
5	APATITE
6	FELDSPAR
7	QUARTZ
8	TOPAZ
9	CORUNDUM
10	DIAMOND

In 1812 the German mineralogist Fredrik Mohs created a relative scale of mineral hardness that is still used today. When a harder mineral (your hammer, with its steel head) hits a softer mineral (calcite), the softer mineral will break. How it breaks is also directly related to the atomic structure. Gemstones are all very hard minerals, valuable because they can be cut and shaped into beautiful forms by metal tools. Talc is so soft that it is ground up and used as baby powder.

GIMME A BREAK!

Cleavage is a smooth, flat break between the layers of atoms in a crystal. The tightness of the atomic bonds is indicated by how the mineral breaks. If it breaks cleanly and easily, the bonds are very tight. If the mineral shatters here and there, the cleavage is good or fair. You can crumble a piece of talc in your hand; its cleavage is poor.

Some minerals, like quartz, have no cleavage: they fracture. A fracture is an uneven break with no relationship to the crystal lattice. Opal is a beautiful gemstone, but its atoms are arranged randomly. It always fractures when hammered.

Tenacity is another property defined by a mineral's atomic bonds. It determines how we use minerals commercially. Native metals such as gold, copper, and silver are used for jewelry because they are malleable—they can be hammered into thin sheets. House wiring is made of copper. Copper is malleable and ductile, meaning it can be drawn out into a thin wire. Copper is also flexible—it can be stretched out of shape and can stay that way—and it is capable of conducting electricity. Platinum is the most ductile of metals. One ounce of platinum, pulled into a thin wire, would stretch from New York City to Omaha, Nebraska!

Asbestos (above) has an extremely splintery fracture, while graphite (below), which is used for pencil lead, has an uneven fracture. Both have poor cleavage.

TWISTED INTO CRYSTALS

All of these properties of minerals rely on the combination of elements that makes them unique. The interaction of each element's electrons also determines the ultimate shape of the mineral, its crystal form. Minerals can assume an infinite variety of crystal forms, based on their crystal lattice. Crystallographers, people who study crystal forms, have grouped the shapes into thirty-two different categories. These categories are arranged

Pyrite, sometimes known as fool's gold, is found in varied forms, two of which are pictured above, the cube (left) and a "star," which was found in shale.

FROZEN MOMENTS

Inclusions happen when a mineral forms around another substance. Pieces of amber, an organic mineral made of compressed tree resin, frequently have bugs and plants trapped inside. Air and water are common inclusions in many minerals, but even grass seeds have been found trapped in quartz crystals! Phantom crystals occur when one crystal is trapped inside a larger, opaque crystal. The phantom looks like a faint, ghostly image.

under six major classes, called crystal systems. While most minerals have a single crystal form, some minerals are polymorphic. They don't have a set shape. Depending on the heat and pressure exerted when they formed, they can have any of many crystal forms. Pyrite is a polymorphic mineral because it can form in perfect cubes, in shapes like pancakes, and in rounded blobs.

Transparent crystals have some interesting optical properties. Depending on the crystal form, the length of a crystal may often

GOOD VIBRATIONS

In 1880, Pierre and Jacques Curie discovered that if you applied pressure to one end of a quartz crystal, a voltage could be measured on certain flat sides, or faces, of the crystal. They called this effect piezoelectricity.

If you apply electricity to a quartz crystal it squeezes the crystal, making it vibrate very quickly. By the 1920s, researchers discovered that the constant 32,768 cycles-per-second frequency of a squeezed quartz crystal could be used to keep perfect time in a clock. The quartz watch soon followed, as did radio transmitters and receivers. Thin plates of quartz, vibrating thousands of times per second, ensure that your favorite radio station always stays at the same frequency. Although quartz used commercially is now grown in laboratories, it is still a valuable and important commodity. Quartz is used to filter, amplify, and control electricity in devices ranging from complex naval navigation systems to your home computer.

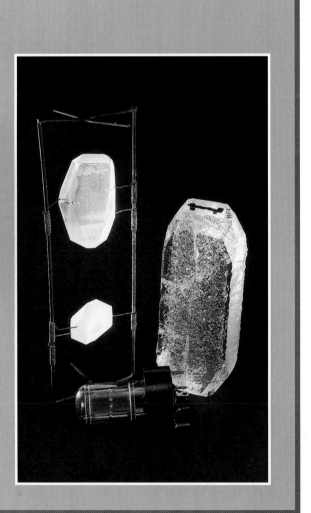

be different from its width. This difference defines the way the crystal transmits or refracts light. In singly refractive (isotropic) crystals, light moves in the same speed in every direction within the crystal. Doubly refractive, or birefringent, crystals split light into two. The light waves then move at different speeds and in different directions, transmitting a double image through the mineral.

Iceland spar calcite and ulexite both show excellent birefringence. Isotropic crystals were once set in the decks of ships to transmit light to the dark galleys below.

Some crystals show different colors depending on which way you hold the mineral. This effect, pleochroism, occurs when a birefringent crystal absorbs light unequally from different directions. A mineral that shows two different colors (depending on the angle you hold it at) is dichromatic. The Vikings used cordierite, a dichromatic crystal, to navigate on cloudy days. The navigator would hold the transparent crystal and turn it until it changed color to a violet-blue. When it turned color, he could tell which direction the sun was, shining polarized light through the crystal. Trichromatic crystals, showing three different colors, can also occur.

CRYSTAL SYMMETRY

Slice a crystal through its center, and both pieces will look like mirror images of each other. This is called symmetry. Much of the beauty and magic of crystals come from their symmetry.

Even though it may look as if a crystal is symmetrical, it may not be. Chemical and physical tests can determine whether a mineral's crystal structure is symmetrical. Nonsymmetrical crystals have some unusual properties. Piezoelectric crystals generate

CRYSTAL MAGIC

Belief in crystal healing dates back to the Middle Ages, when people thought that the purity of gemstones could protect them from disease. Crystals were ground into powders and given as medicine, sometimes killing the patient!

Those who could afford to do so wore gems to stave off the Black Death—the bubonic plague that ravaged Europe. Even the varnish on Stradivarius violins contains finely ground gemstones, thought to suppress unpleasant high frequencies of sound.

21

electricity when squeezed or bent. Pyroelectric crystals generate electricity when heated.

GETTING INTO THE HABIT

Some minerals have no obvious crystal form. Amorphous minerals, such as opal and limonite, look blobby. Tiny crystals can grow so close together that they blend into a single mass of rock. Polymorphic minerals don't have a consistent shape. Depending on the heat and pressure exerted when they formed, polymorphic minerals can have any of many crystal forms. And certain crystals always grow in twins, or pairs. Twinned crystals may be penetrating twins, which grow through each other. They may be contact twins, which are joined at the bottom, or repeated crystals, which grow together like saltines in a wrapper.

As crystals join together in clusters, they grow into fantastic and unusual shapes. These special shapes—the mineral's habit, or pattern of growth—give us more clues for identifying minerals. Iron and nickel crystals can form dendrites, creeping outward like tree limbs. Garnet crystals are equidimensional, with the same diameter in every direction. Other minerals form crystals that are broad, flat blades or long, sharp needles.

The word *crystal* comes from the Greek *krystallos*, meaning "clear ice," like the quartz points that the ancient Greeks found as they mined lead, silver, and copper. *Crystal* also evokes images of beauty—deep blue sapphires, sparkling diamonds—minerals that express their crystal structure on the surface with crystal faces and perfect geometric forms. Yet even the ugliest mineral has a crystal form, an underlying lattice of whirling electrons, a special arrangement of atoms that makes it unique.

A COLORFUL EQUATION 3

As electrons whirl in their orbits, they give many qualities to each mineral. While crystal forms emerge from the pattern of the atoms, it is the unique chemical composition of each mineral that sets its most striking visual features.

THE BASIS OF COLOR

Color is the most obvious characteristic of a mineral. Some minerals have consistent coloration, like gold, silver, copper, and emerald. Other minerals come in a rainbow of different colors.

These amethyst crystals are a color variation of quartz.

Color in minerals comes from several sources. The interaction of light with the atoms in the crystal form is the basis of a mineral's color. The crystal form absorbs some wavelengths of light, and reflects the others. The reflected wavelength is the color you see. Minerals that have one consistent color defined by their

23

chemical composition, like the native elements, are idochromatic. Sulfur is an idochromatic mineral; it always looks yellow.

Even though rubies and sapphires share the same chemical composition, they come in very different colors, with many hues. These minerals are allochromatic. Their color comes from trace impurities of other elements. These impurities are so small that they aren't included in the mineral's chemical formula, but the slightest hint of an impurity can create a unique color in a mineral.

MANY COLORS, ONE MINERAL. Quartz is such a common mineral that it has been given many special names based on its color. Impurities in quartz generate the most obvious color differences. Here are just a few:

Name	Color	Impurities
rock crystal	transparent	no impurities
amethyst	purple	iron oxide
citrine	yellow-orange	iron oxide
rose quartz	cloudy pink	titanium, iron
smoky quartz	brownish-black	uranium, aluminum

MANY MINERALS, ONE COLOR.

Purplish-pink minerals often contain atoms of manganese. These are a few minerals that rely on manganese for their hues of red, violet, and pink: rhodonite, red beryl, biotite, tremolite, tourmaline, and morganite.

Yet manganese causes andalusite to be green! So impurities aren't consistent in coloring allochromatic minerals. It's the unique interaction between each crystal form and each impurity that creates vibrant color in minerals.

Citrine, rough, and cut and polished

COLORING WITH MINERALS

From the days of the first cave paintings, minerals played a crucial role in the way people expressed themselves with color. When minerals erode, pigments are released into the surrounding earth. The pigmented earth is mined and used to color the wax in crayons and the liquid bases of paints and inks.

Pigment mining is a big business. One mine in Hiwassee, Virginia, is currently the world's only source of the color sienna. All of North America's ocher comes from a mining operation in Cartersville, Georgia. Titanium is used for the most common color in paints— white. North America's largest titanium mine is in Quebec, Canada. Many earth-tone colors come from iron ore minerals.

Raw umber is a colorful mix of yellow goethite and black magnetite pigments. Variations of goethite also produce sienna and ocher pigments. Red iron oxide comes from hematite, a dark black iron ore. To create "burnt" colors, like burnt sienna, pigmented earth is heated. This alters its chemical composition, changing its color.

Minerals are essential to coloration. White titanium and zinc oxide are painted on the walls of your house. Cobalt adds a bluish hue to dishes and glasses. Sienna ends up in dyes coloring envelopes and folders. Mineral pigments color tiles, cement, bricks, and other building materials.

Metal ions are the primary sources of color in minerals. Copper often causes greens and blues. Iron frequently creates red and yellow hues. Chromium creates many colors, including red in rubies, emerald green in beryl, and purple or red in alexandrite.

SCRATCHING THE SURFACE

A mineral's true color is a tricky thing to determine. A mineral may look brown to your eyes, but only one factor will tell you its consistent natural pigmentation: the mineral's streak. Streak testing, by rubbing a mineral against a dry ceramic surface, helps us identify like-colored minerals. A brown mineral may have a golden streak, or a brown streak, or an orange streak. A piece of natural chalk leaves a white streak on a blackboard. In the 1500s, the British discovered that graphite, a carbon mineral, would make marks on paper. Now, when you write with a pencil, you leave a streak of graphite behind.

This streak test shows the true color of hematite (left) and malachite.

The visual surface texture of a mineral is called its luster. No matter whether a mineral is transparent, translucent, or opaque, it will have a distinctive luster. The luster of copper is metallic, which may be shiny and reflective, or dull. Sulfur has a resinous luster and looks yellowish and glossy. Glossy white and slightly iridescent, talc's luster is pearly. Asbestos has a silky luster, like smooth fibers.

OPTICAL ILLUSIONS

Light can play tricks with the surface of a mineral. Reflection of light makes the mineral's surface look slick and glossy. Refraction of light makes the surface color of the mineral change in different spots, depending on how you hold it. Together, they form a schiller. Labradorescence is one type of schiller that shows up on the surface of labradorite. It looks like oil on water, or a soap bubble. Another schiller is opalescence, named for opal, a shimmering play of many colors across the surface of the mineral.

Tigereye quartz demonstrates chatoyancy. The word's origin is the French chatoyer, *which means to shine like a cat's eye.*

Inclusions of other minerals and microscopic cavities in a mineral's surface can cause other striking visual effects. Chatoyancy makes a mineral look like the eye of a cat. Tigereye quartz, caused by tiny needles of asbestos trapped in the crystal, has this cat's-eye effect. Minerals with adularescence, like moonstone, show a shimmering surface by reflecting light from cavities too small to see.

Asterism is a starburst shape highly prized in gemstones. It comes from inclusions of tiny crystals that lie in a crisscross pattern in the mineral. Needles of the mineral rutile cause this effect in rubies and sapphires, causing them to display a glowing star on the surface of the stone. Coatings of tiny crystals growing on top of other crystals can cause iridescence, a beautiful rainbow of colors on a mineral's surface.

GLOWING STONES

Not only can minerals transmit and reflect light, some emit light as well. Minerals are called luminescent if they emit light under some sort of stress that excites the mineral's electrons.

Photoluminescent minerals glow when light hits them. Ultraviolet light excites the electrons in some minerals, making them fluorescent, glowing in vivid colors. If the mineral keeps glowing after the ultraviolet light source is shut off, it's phosphorescent. It can continue to release trapped electrons for minutes, hours, and sometimes weeks!

Cathodoluminescence is the basis for television and computer screens, since some minerals glow when you shoot a steady stream of electrons at them, as in a cathode ray tube (CRT). Radioluminescence happens when some minerals are bombarded with radium or X rays.

Minerals that glow when scratched or crunched are triboluminescent, as are wintergreen Life Savers when you crunch them between your teeth. If you heat a mineral and it glows, it's thermoluminescent. Other minerals, if splashed with or immersed in certain chemicals, will glow from the reaction between the chemical bonds.

A unique chemical stew bubbled inside each mineral as it formed, making it different from its neighbors. Not only does its

GO WITH THE GLOW

Fluorescence is the most common type of mineral luminescence. About 15 percent of all minerals fluoresce.

But why can one piece of calcite glow white under an ultraviolet lamp, while another piece glows deep red, and a third piece doesn't glow at all?

Fluorescence occurs because of certain chemicals, called activators, which excite ions in the minerals. When the chemical is a part of the structure of the mineral, it's an intrinsic activator. When an impurity causes the fluorescence, it's an impurity activator.

Minerals with a metallic luster never fluoresce. And a mineral containing even one percent iron, copper, nickel, or cobalt will not fluoresce. These metallics are quenchers, since they extinguish any potential fluorescence in a mineral, canceling out the effect of an activator.

Mineral fluorescence was first noticed in the lighting generated by sparks flying from welding equipment in zinc mines. Miners learned to recognize the zinc ore willemite by its brilliant greenish-yellow fluorescence and lengthy phosphorescence.

In the 1930s, ultraviolet (UV) lamps were developed for use in medicine and to prospect for minerals. Tungsten was an important mineral during World War II, used for aircraft and armaments. Scheelite, a tungsten ore, fluoresced bright blue under UV light, so prospectors used the lamps to discover tungsten deposits.

By the 1950s, prospectors used UV lamps to look for uranium in the deserts of the southwestern United States. In more recent times, mineral collectors use UV lamps to find fluorescent mineral specimens.

The world's largest concentration of fluorescent minerals is around Franklin, New Jersey, where over eighty-two different types of fluorescent minerals are found! Two museums show off this bounty of glowing stones: the Franklin Mineral Museum and the Sterling Hill Mining Museum. An exhibit of fluorescent minerals from the Sterling Hill Mine is also in the Smithsonian Institution.

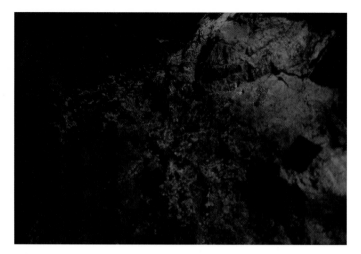

Fluorescent willemite and calcite. Many natural history museums have displays of these eerily glowing minerals.

base chemical composition affect how a mineral looks, but so do many other factors. Trace elements can change a clear calcite to blue, or make it capable of fluorescence. Tiny inclusions of other minerals can cause asterism. A surface eroded or coated with other crystals can cause odd plays of light across the mineral.

Each mineral is remarkable, expressing its colorful equation as a feast for the eyes—a visual delight.

THE MANY FACES OF FELDSPAR

Feldspar is the world's most common mineral. It's the chief ingredient of many igneous and metamorphic rocks. Depending on its color, crystal form, chemical composition, and the way it reflects light, feldspar may have any of many different names. Some glossy feldspars, such as labradorite, moonstone, and sunstone, are cut into gemstones.

Weathered feldspars form an important metamorphic mineral, kaolin clay. It's used to make plates, dishes, bowls, and other ceramics. Feldspar is also an important ingredient in glassware. If you look around your bathroom, you'll find it's full of feldspar: the toilet bowl, ceramic tiles, paints, plastics, and even cleansers contain feldspar.

4

MAKING A DEPOSIT

Minerals are the building blocks of rocks. To determine how minerals grow, we need to take a close look at how the rocks that contain them formed.

MINERALS FROM MAGMA

Metallic deposits tend to form in ancient igneous rock, deep under the earth's surface. In some places, minerals fill the spaces in eroded igneous rock when magma replaces weakened material. These intrusive igneous deposits may contain a single mineral, such as magnetite, or may contain many different minerals. Each mineral crystallizes from the magma at a different temperature. One region in Bingham, New Mexico, shows minerals depositing like the layers of an onion. As the pool of magma cooled, zinc minerals formed around a core of copper minerals, with denser lead and silver minerals growing as an outer layer.

North America's largest metallic deposits are in igneous rock. When a gigantic pool of magma solidifies underground, it creates a pluton, filled with many useful minerals. The Canadian Shield is a massive pluton that stretches from Great Slave Lake in the Northwest Territories to eastern Quebec and New England. From

Arizona and New Mexico up into Montana, the remains of ancient volcanoes can be seen. Both regions are rich in gold, silver, nickel, copper, platinum, iron, titanium, and other important metals. Some minerals only grow within certain types of rocks. These minerals are said to be associated with their host rock.

Mineral	Rock
diamond	kimberlite
platinum	dunite, peridotite
chromite	peridotite, serpentine
ilmenite	anorthosite, gabbro
nickel sulfide	gabbro, norite
tin	granite
beryl	granite pegmatite

Water, superheated by magma, can also carry igneous mineral deposits through the earth. When the water cools, minerals deposit in crevices. This hydrothermal action is responsible for creating veins of minerals. Superheated water can also erode soft rock and replace it with minerals. A vast region of limestone in the Mississippi valley contains deposits of lead and zinc ore, where hydrothermal deposits intruded into the sedimentary rock.

Certain geologic formations actively generate minerals. Gases belching from volcano craters deposit crystals of casserite (tin ore), sulfur, cobalt, lead, zinc, copper, bismuth, and phosphorus. Magnetite, hematite, pyrite, lead, zinc, copper, and other minerals fall out of the steam from fumaroles—volcanic vents that channel steam and gases from deep within the earth. Crystals of boron, arsenic, gold, silver, lead, zinc, and cinnabar grow on the walls of hot springs.

EARTH BURPS

Gases bubbling from deep within the earth can change the chemical composition of limestone beds, forming new rocks and minerals. When invaded by these gases, carbonate rocks change into silicate rocks. The result is a skarn formation, a deposit rich in crystalline garnet and other interesting crystals.

As magma pushes to the earth's surface, it forms its own plumbing system, melting the rock in its path. Dikes are magma pipes that rise vertically to the earth's surface. Sills are sheets of magma that flow horizontally between layers of rock. Because of the wealth of minerals formed by magma, dikes and sills are great places to look for mineral growth.

PEGMATITES

Pegmatite dikes are a rich, complex mix of minerals. A single pegmatite can extend for thousands of feet. The magma in a pegmatite cooled slowly, creating massive crystals that can be hundreds of feet long and weigh many tons. A single spodumene crystal found in a South Dakota pegmatite was 42 feet (12.8

Emeralds are a rich green variation of beryl. These are from Boyacá, Colombia.

meters) long, 5 feet (1.5 meters) wide, and weighed more than 90 tons. These large crystals have many spaces between them, where subsequent magma intrusions and hydrothermal deposits added smaller, rarer crystals. Uranium minerals (including rare earths, minerals that are oxides of the rare earth elements at the upper end of the periodic table) and gemstones can form in pegmatite dikes.

All of these minerals are found in one small pegmatite dike in Ontario: garnet, smoky quartz, amethyst, milky quartz, albite, amazonite, peristerite, clevelandite, biotite, microcline, perthite, monazite, beryl, aquamarine, emerald, heliodor, allanite, lyndochite, columbite, apatite, tourmaline, fluorite, and zircon.

Some of the world's most beautiful gemstones are mined from pegmatite dikes: tourmaline from Pala, California; fluorite from the Wise Mine, New Hampshire; amazonite from Amelia, Virginia; emeralds from Minas Geras, Brazil. Brazil has the earth's largest expanse of pegmatite dikes, scattered across 72,000 square miles (186,480 kilometers) of jungle.

FUEL FOR THOUGHT

In the sedimentary process, layers of matter settle and compress into rock. Some organic materials—bones, sea shells—became limestone. Other organic remains settled into mud and slowly decayed. Pockets of gases and natural oils, released from the decaying remains, became trapped in the mud. As the mud compressed into shale, a sedimentary rock, these pockets formed hydrocarbons: petroleum and natural gas. These oils and gases floated into crevices and fissures between masses of rock, or soaked into the pores of the shale and sandstone. Hydrocarbons are only found in sedimentary rocks.

Decaying plant matter goes through a similar compression process to turn into coal. When plants decompose underwater, it slows their rate of decay, trapping (or "fixing") and compressing essential amounts of carbon. The percentage of carbon and the amount of recognizable plant matter remaining determine what we call the substance:

Peat-cutting on the Isle of Skye, Scotland.

- Peat is the first step in the process. It is cut from bogs for use as fuel and fertilizer. It contains very little fixed carbon, and up to 9 percent water.

- Lignite (also called brown coal) is more compact than peat, but never has more than 50 percent fixed carbon. It's crumbly when dried, and is used as a fuel.

- Bituminous coal contains up to 80 percent fixed carbon. Shiny bituminous coal burns better than duller coal, which often contains clay and gases.

- Anthracite coal contains 90 percent or more fixed carbon. It burns cleanly. It formed in regions where mountain-building processes deeply compressed the original sedimentary deposits. Pennsylvania contains the world's largest deposits of anthracite coal.

Coal, oil, and natural gas are the cornerstones of our energy systems, providing heating, transportation, and electricity for hun-

We don't usually think that water can evaporate underground, but it does, leaving behind minerals like aragonite spikes (left) and rhodochrosite cubes.

dreds of millions of people around the world. Eighty percent of the electricity in the United States comes from burning fossil fuels. These fossil fuels can replenish themselves—peat keeps turning to lignite, and lignite to coal—but the process repeats very slowly. We will eventually run out of these fossil fuels because we consume them more quickly than they can develop.

THE POWER OF WATER

Water is an essential part of the earth, and is responsible for many of the earth's mineral deposits. As rainwater soaks into the ground, it carries along trace amounts of chemicals and minerals. Carbonic acid, from decaying leaves, makes the water capable of eroding soft limestone deep below the earth's surface. The water runs along natural slopes in the bedrock, widening the joints and the bedding planes, the separations between the layers of limestone. Cavities open up, leaving a space for mineral deposition to occur.

As sediment-laden water evaporates underground, it leaves behind the minerals it carries. This process creates the amazing formations we see in caverns, and builds smaller assemblages of crystals as well. Minerals attach themselves to every crevice: hollows from erosion, or vugs caused by the bursting of gas bubbles in igneous rock. These pockets of minerals often contain the showiest crystals: spikes of aragonite, cubes of rhodochrosite and fluorite, splinters of barite, and pointy dogtooth calcite crystals. Geodes, which form around vugs, contain minerals, oil, or beautiful crystals inside. Evaporation of water can also leave vast sedimentary mineral deposits behind. Where salty inland seas once covered the Midwest, there are now regions coated with layers of gypsum, anhydrite, halite, and potash.

GOLD FEVER

The California gold rush of 1849 happened after James Marshall found placer gold at Sutter's Mill. Over 200,000 people poured westward, seeking their fortune. Some enterprising prospectors followed the streams from Sutter's Mill up into the Sierra Nevada mountains to their source, finding the "mother lode" of gold veins in quartz. In less than five years, most of the placer nuggets and flakes had been scooped up, and miners turned to the tougher job of prospecting underground for gold veins.

MIGHTY MORPHING MINERALS

Some elements in minerals easily give up their places to others during metamorphic processes. Pseudomorphs occur when one mineral replaces another, but the new mineral retains some of the characteristics of the original. These chameleons of the mineral world masquerade so well it's difficult to figure out what they are.

Paramorphs occur when a mineral's chemical composition doesn't change, but its crystal structure does, and the mineral doesn't gain or lose any matter. Very slowly, aragonite can change to calcite.

Alteration pseudomorphs either gain or lose an element to create a new mineral. When water evaporates out of gypsum, anhydrite crystals remain. The loss of antimony from discrazite creates native silver.

Replacement (or substitution) pseudomorphs happen when the original substance is completely replaced by a new mineral. Petrified wood and other fossilized objects are pseudomorphs. Limonite, a crumbly iron ore, can replace thicker iron pyrite in cubes.

Encrustation paramorphs are coatings of one type of mineral on top of an original mineral, which may no longer exist. This can alter the shape of the new mineral: rose quartz crystals growing on top of anhydrite look like rock candy.

By heating or irradiating minerals, people can create intentional mineral pseudomorphs. Both amethyst and citrine are quartz with trace

amounts of iron. Amethyst is more common than citrine. To create citrine, amethyst can be heated until it turns yellow. Many gemstones are irradiated to bring out deeper colors, making them more valuable.

As hot lava enters the ocean at Wa'ahula, on Kilauea, Hawaii, bathers stand on a beach of black lava sand.

Dissolved minerals in water can replace natural matter, creating objects frozen in time. Petrified forests occurred when tree trunks were trapped underwater and buried in layers of ash-laden sediment that prevented rotting. The silica from the ash, dissolved in the water, seeped into the tree tissue and replaced it with quartz. Similarly, the slowly decaying remains of creatures buried in ancient sea sediments had silica seep into their pores as sandstone and limestone formed. The remains of the plant or animal were trapped in stone, creating a fossil.

Water can carry minerals for long distances. Placer minerals are those found scattered far from their original source. These include gold flakes and gold nuggets in river bottoms. Loose gemstones scattered in soft clay are also placer deposits, like the rubies and sapphires found in North Carolina, Montana, Sri Lanka, and Burma. Placer minerals in these areas probably came from mountains that eroded away ages ago. In other areas, glaciers transported placers thousands of miles. Michigan's Upper Peninsula contains massive copper nuggets dropped by glaciers.

Ocean beaches also contain placers, where heavy minerals collect in the sand. Beaches in Nome, Alaska, contain grains of gold; the black sand beaches of Hawaii are mostly magnetite. Diamonds, carried down the Orange River and dumped into the sea, wash up on the shores of Alexander Bay in South Africa. Twenty-five percent of the world's titanium comes from the black sand beaches of New South Wales, Australia. Like giant vacuum cleaners, dredges suck up the sand and extract tiny crystals of ilmenite and rutile, both important titanium ores.

Placer deposits are mysterious. It's not always possible to pinpoint the origin of a placer mineral. But it's often easy to find them. These heavier minerals carried in water tend to accumulate in stream bottoms, below boulders and other obstructions, and along inner curves as the stream flows toward the sea.

Wherever the earth makes a deposit, minerals grow. Using our knowledge of how rocks form, we can make educated guesses as to where to find the minerals we're looking for.

5
TRACKING HIDDEN TREASURE

How does a prospector know where to pan for gold? How does an oil company know where to drill for oil? How does a mineral collector know where to find fluorite?

The search for minerals is a special type of detective work. Geologic formations provide the clues, since they show us the nature of the underlying rock. A geologist is a master sleuth in the hunt, determining the origins and placement of minerals.

TRICKS OF THE TRADE

Geologists use special tools to probe formations for clues to their origins. Magnetometers measure magnetism, indicating pockets of magnetic iron ore. Geiger counters crackle when they sense radiation, the emission of particles from radium-bearing minerals. Gravimeters measure the difference in gravity over small sections of land, which tells the variation in density of the rocks underfoot. Electrical surveys uncover ore deposits by noting a change in the expected current flow from one point to another. Seismic surveys bounce shock waves against underground formations, which can be measured to show layers of different types of rock. When a deposit is found, a drill hole is bored to take samples of rock.

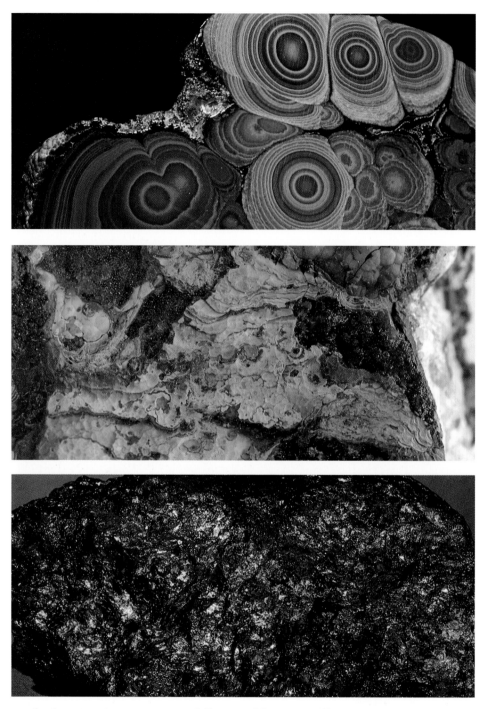

Malachite (top), azurite (middle), and bornite all contain copper, which causes their blue-green color.

These samples will determine whether the rock is suitable to be mined.

ALL IN THE FAMILY

Families of minerals, related by chemical composition, tend to deposit together. Where you see malachite (a green copper mineral), you'll also probably find azurite (a blue copper mineral), and bornite (a multicolored copper mineral). There are 165 different copper-bearing minerals in all, and when you find one, you'll find others nearby. The same holds true for other families of minerals. Amethyst, rock crystal quartz, and citrine tend to form together. Most varieties of feldspar grow in close association to each other. Soft zeolite minerals—silicates that contain water—often occur together in igneous rock vugs.

ACCESSORIES

All rocks contain an essential recipe of minerals, but some rocks may also contain accessory minerals. These crystals formed in association with the basic minerals. They include many gemstones and minerals used in industry. Granite is often a source of pyrite, tourmaline, and zircon. Beryl, spodumene, and topaz—all beautiful gemstones—may be found in granite pegmatites. Limestone can contain garnets and talc.

Although not chemically related, there are other minerals that grow in association with each other. Veins of native metals—gold, silver, and copper—form inside veins of quartz, as do crystals of tourmaline. Native metals also tend to grow together. Metallic ores often contain multiple metals in a single rock. Titanium and iron are frequently found together, as are lead and zinc, and chromium and platinum. Copper, gold, and molybdenum grow in association with each other. So do tin and tungsten.

SURFACE CLUES

All rocks tell a story. By carefully observing the rocks lying on the surface, you can connect them to your knowledge of how miner-

als deposit. Road cuts are a great place to examine rocks. You can see the strata, or layers, showing different types of rock. Anticlines and synclines are formations that show the folding of the rocks during metamorphic processes. Along these folds, you may find crystals formed by contact metamorphism. Other crevices and cracks can hide depositional crystals.

In sedimentary rocks, slate, shale, and mudstone point to possible fossils. Sandstone traps liquids—water, petroleum, and brine (containing salt)—and may contain fossils. Limestone might contain metallic deposits, fossils, or crystals in crevices and vugs. On a leafy forest floor, you can guess that a pegmatite dike might be nearby if you see big quartz boulders, graphic granite (quartz and granite intermixed) and mica growing in thick books (lots of pieces of mica all stuck together). Many old mica

The dramatic folds in the rock are easily visible in this road cut along Interstate 68 in Sideling Hill, Maryland. Some books specialize in roadside geology.

mines in North Carolina contain pegmatite dikes that were ignored by the miners, who only wanted the mica, used extensively in electronics.

MINERALOGY: UNDERSTANDING MINERALS

Mineralogists are the scientists who study the nature of minerals. The roots of mineralogy date back to early philosophers. A pupil of Aristotle, Theophrastus, wrote *The Book of Stones* sometime before 300 B.C. It was the first-ever book about minerals. He grouped minerals into categories, such as metals, stones, and earths.

Growing up in a busy mining district of Saxony, Germany, Georgius Agricola (1494–1555) carefully studied minerals and wrote *De Re Metallica*, a book considered to be the foundation of modern mineralogy. René Descartes, Henkel Becher, Marie Curie, and many other scientists contributed to the knowledge of mineral formation and properties through their work. Centuries of studies at the Harvard Mineralogical Museum, the Smithsonian Museum of Natural History, and countless other museums have added immeasurably to what we now know about minerals and how they form.

The first school devoted to mineral study, the Mining Academy of Freiburg, Germany, was founded in 1765 and remained open for over 150 years. Modern mineral education is still tied closely to mining, since the applied knowledge of minerals leads to finding new uses for the elements locked inside them. Today's major centers of mineral education are the Colorado School of Mines, the Missouri School of Mines, and the École des Mines in Paris. There are now many such important mineralogical institutions around the world.

SPECIAL INDICATORS

A careful look at plant life can also tell you about mineral deposits. Gypsum, chalk, and potash cause soil to be alkaline, providing a comfortable environment for certain plant species. A high concentration of metals causes a unique set of plant life to develop, since metals are highly poisonous to many species. Salt licks are generally bare spots in the forest, where plants can't grow. Knowing it would make the farmers' fields useless, Roman invaders sprinkled salt on the ground around Carthage to prevent the city from being rebuilt.

The field of geobotany explores the connections between geologic deposits and plants. Prospectors have been using plants as indicators to deposits since the days of the Roman Empire, when it was known that certain plants grew atop natural reservoirs, water sources deep underground. In the seventeenth century, Scandinavian miners used the wildflower *Lychinis Alpina* to locate deposits of iron pyrite. Prospectors in the 1850s looked for locoweed in the deserts of the southwestern United States, as it grew in association with selenite, an important indicator of uranium ore. Bladder campion, a colorful wildflower, flourishes around zinc deposits.

Magnetic iron ore can be located by using a compass. In the districts bordering the New York–New Jersey state line near Ringwood, New Jersey, where iron was mined in Colonial times, deposits of magnetite make it almost impossible to use a compass for hiking. In fact, prospectors used to use a compass to find the ore deposits. Each deposit is like a giant magnet, and it will repel or attract the opposite pole of the compass needle. Prospectors would walk around and watch the behavior of the compass, determining the position of the ore deposit based on when the compass needle settled firmly between the two poles.

A Geiger counter will measure the amount of radiation emitted from a mineral deposit. In the early days of uranium prospecting, prospectors would set an unexposed roll of film on a suspect piece of ground. If uranium ore was nearby, the X rays emitted from the ore would expose the film. The prospector would return and look at the film. If it had foggy images on it, the prospector knew there were uranium ores underfoot.

Some minerals can be found by using your sense of smell. Sulfur stinks like rotten eggs. Clay, especially thick kaolin clay used for pottery making, has a distinct earthy smell. Poisonous arsenic minerals smell like garlic.

WHAT'S IN A NAME?

Sometimes the name of a mineral can be a clue as to its origin and how to find it. Some minerals are named for the places they were first found, such as vesuvianite (for Italy's Mount Vesuvius), franklinite (Franklin, New Jersey), and anapaite (Anapa, Russia). Since Mount Vesuvius is a volcano, you might guess that vesuvianite will be found in deposits of igneous rock.

Some mineral names capture bits of the language of the people who named them, like halite (*hals*, Greek for "salt") and albite (*alba*, Latin for "white"). Knowing a little bit of Latin and Greek can go a long way toward mineral identification. Albite is a white feldspar. Halite is salt, and tastes and smells like it!

Still other minerals are named for the people who discovered them, like smithsonite (James Smithson, founder of the Smithsonian Institution), goethite (Johann Wolfgang von Goethe, German poet and amateur mineralogist), and prehnite (Colonel von Prehnis, Netherlands).

At least a dozen new minerals are discovered every year. The people who make the discovery get to pick a name, which is sent to a board of mineralogists for approval. New mineral names often honor people who contributed greatly to mineralogy in the past, such as kunzite, named for George Kunz, an author and a vice president of Tiffany and Company, a large jewelry firm in New York City.

Associations, indicators, and surface rocks all give clues to where mineral deposits can be found. Once a mineral deposit is suspected, geologists use additional tests to determine if it is good enough to be mined. Mineral collectors use the same clues to pinpoint good sites to find nice mineral specimens.

BELOW THE SALT

Salt is an essential mineral for human survival. In ancient times, salt was considered a treasure worth more than gold. The word *salary* comes from the Latin *salarium* (salt money), since Roman soldiers received some of their pay in salt. Noblemen frequently "salted away" their mineral riches in vaults, and would show their disfavor of guests at the table by seating them "below the salt," far away from the precious commodity. While massive evaporate flats of salt—both in deserts and along shorelines—have served as sources of salt, most salt mining now occurs underground.

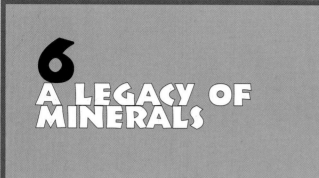

6
A LEGACY OF MINERALS

Human history is cast in terms of minerals: the Stone Age, the Bronze Age, and the Iron Age. From the very beginning, we've tapped these precious resources. The first uses were obvious: caves for shelter, and weapons and tools of stone. Paleolithic (meaning "old stone" in Greek) peoples, roaming the earth between 100,000 and 7000 B.C., used natural ocher pigments to create paintings in their caverns. They struck chips of flint together, and found fire. Neolithic ("new stone") peoples discovered that clay, shaped and dried in the sun, would make pottery, sculpture, tiles, and bricks. Museum treasures around the world tell us of these peoples through their mineral creations.

By 4000 B.C., the first large civilizations appeared, working magic with native metals and using stone to capture the written word. The Sumerians recorded their daily transactions on clay tablets. The Egyptians carved elaborate hieroglyphics in stone, and used tiny chips of limestone, called ostraca, to scribble quick notes on. Gemstones and gold became symbols of wealth and prosperity. For over two thousand years, Egyptian engineers and prospectors ranged across hundreds of miles looking for these elusive treasures. They found turquoise in the Sinai Peninsula, agate along the Nile River, and gold in the Sudan. Starting as early as 1925 B.C., they sank mining shafts up to 800 feet (244 meters) deep along the shores of the Red Sea, where men descended by ladder to dig for emeralds.

Soft copper became the first metal shaped into tools. Easily melted, liquid copper could be poured into molds to make spear and axe blades. By melting different metals together, metalsmiths discovered alloys, which were stronger than any one individual metal. The Bronze Age dawned about 3000 B.C., when Phoenician sailors brought cassiterite (tin ore) from the British Isles to Greece and Egypt. The tin ore was combined with copper from Cyprus to make bronze. The Greeks favored bronze for weapons and armor. The Romans worked with galena (lead ore), creating polished cups and dishes. The first coins, crafted of silver and gold stamped with special designs, simplified trade between cities. Through their artifacts, many early civilizations showed amazing abilities to work with molten metals. Platinum melts at 3,225°F (1,774°C), yet platinum ornaments have been found in archeological digs in Peru.

Smelting (the art of extracting liquid metal from rocks with metallic ores) soon progressed to the point that iron could be worked. This ushered in

This magnificent point was made by flaking small pieces of obsidian away with another rock. Obsidian is a natural glass, and its edges can be quite sharp.

STORIES IN STONE

During the nineteenth century, lithography (a method of creating prints from original art) relied on a special smooth, soft-grained limestone from a quarry in Solnhofen, Bavaria, in Germany. So the sheets of stone would be perfect, workers used hand tools to carefully slice the sheets of limestone from the quarry walls. Because of this delicate process, an unexpected bounty was uncovered for naturalists: a perfect fossil record from a shallow prehistoric lagoon. These stories in stone have given us an unexpected glimpse into the past. Among the excellent fossils collected from this quarry are examples of *Pterosaurus*, a large flying reptile, and *Compsognathus*, a tiny dinosaur. Most importantly, the quarry contained the only known specimens of *Archaeopteryx*, a curious winged species that might be the link between dinosaurs and birds.

the Iron Age, around 1000 B.C. Since iron was initially so difficult to work with, it was thought to hold magic. The belief was so strong that the Etruscans refused to allow the conquered Romans to forge weapons of iron.

Because of the vast availability of iron ore and the strength of cast iron, iron tools became a part of everyday life. Farmers used them to cultivate fields. Hunters used them to capture their dinners. Sculptors used them to carve marble.

Iron continues to be the world's most important metal. We use it in steel, to build bridges and buildings. When we talk about metal tools, they're almost always made of iron or steel. Since more than 5 percent of the earth's crust is iron ore, we have vast supplies of iron to meet the rising consumption of this common, but significant, metal.

Simple Alloys
brass = copper + zinc
bronze = copper + tin
pewter = copper + tin + antimony
steel = iron + carbon + zinc

From the jade figurines of the second dynasty of China to the jeweled headdresses of the ancient Egyptians and the treasures of the Spanish silver mines of Hannibal, precious metals and gemstones are woven deeply into the fabric of history. But what about their uses today?

You are constantly surrounded by the end products of minerals. When you wake up in the morning and flip on a light switch, the electricity flows through copper wires, from a power plant that may use coal or uranium to produce electricity. Even hydroelectric power, generated by running water, requires metal turbines to generate electricity. The light bulb itself is made from silica, copper, aluminum, tungsten, and trona, all industrial mineral products.

This ornament was in Tutankhamen's tomb. The scarab (beetle) is made of chalcedony. The other materials include carnelian, lapis lazuli, and glass.

The breakfast on your plate came from a farm, where metal tools were used to till the soil and ground-up phosphate minerals fertilized the land. The stoneware plate might be made of kaolin. The shirt you are wearing started as a plant grown on a farm (cotton), or as a mixture of chemicals, extracted from minerals. When you brush your teeth, you use toothpaste that contains at least six different minerals.

Whether you use a bus or a car to get to school, you're riding on top of crushed minerals in roadbeds, including the asphalt and cement. Hydrocarbons power the ride. The average car contains hundreds of different minerals, including over 139 pounds of aluminum, 28 pounds of copper, and 20 pounds of zinc! Over half the lead mined in the United States is used in cars, trucks, and buses.

At school, the building is made of building stone, and the glass windows contain silica and limestone. Walls are painted with pigmented zinc oxides. Books were printed on metal printing presses, using clays and mineral pigments in their inks.

Minerals are still used for art, from paints and clay to crystals carved by master artisans. Like Neolithic peoples, we make pottery, tiles, and bricks, and create jewelry from gemstones. Yet our modern appliances—microwaves, computers, televisions—rely on removing rare minerals from the earth in ways our ancestors never could. Sophisticated mining techniques allow us to extract tiny amounts of precious metals economically from the waste piles of nineteenth-century mines, and to use genetically adapted bacteria to find gold.

Rocks and minerals are the bounty of our earth, and it is up to us to remove them carefully and use them wisely. The earth is full of their diverse forms, waiting to be discovered and appreciated: the hidden treasures of the earth.

GLOSSARY

accessory: mineral that forms in association with another mineral

activators: chemicals that excite ions in a mineral

adularescence: visual effect on the surface of a mineral, caused by light reflecting from microscopic cavities

allochromatic: a single color caused by trace impurities in a mineral

alloy: a mixture of two or more types of minerals, of which one is a metal

amorphous: without an orderly arrangement of atoms

anticline: an arch of stratified rock in which the layers dip in two directions down from a crest

association: minerals and rocks that form near each other because similar conditions are needed for their development

asterism: a visual star effect caused by tiny crystals embedded in a mineral

atom: an orderly arrangement of protons, neutrons, and electrons

atomic structure: the arrangement and type of atoms that exist in a particular substance

batholith: a large mass of intrusive igneous rock, where magma solidified in place

bed: a layer of rock lying horizontally

bedding plane: the surface separating two horizontal layers of rock

bedrock: the solid rock layer underneath a layer of soil

birefringence: double refraction, or transmission of a double image

cathodoluminescence: emission of light from a mineral hit by a cathode ray beam

chatoyancy: a visual effect on a mineral's surface, looking like a cat's eye

cleavage: a plane along which a mineral tends to break, between the atoms

compound: a mixture of more than one element

contact metamorphism: the change in rocks caused by intrusive magma heating existing rocks

crystal: a solid with an orderly arrangement of atoms

crystal form: the visible expression of a crystal lattice

crystal lattice: the pattern in which the atoms of a crystal are arranged

deposit: a natural accumulation of minerals

dichromatic: showing pleochroism in two colors

dike: a sheet of igneous rock, filling a fissure by the extrusive flow of magma

electron: a particle inside an atom, containing a negative electrical charge

element: a unique combination of protons, neutrons, and electrons that cannot be broken down by ordinary chemical methods

extrusive: igneous rock that forms on the earth's surface

fluorescence: emission of light from a mineral when placed under ultraviolet light

fracture: a break in a mineral that is not related to the atomic structure

habit: pattern of growth of crystal clusters

hue: a variation on a primary color

hydrothermal deposits: minerals left behind by water or steam heated by magma

idochromatic: a single color defined by the chemical formula of a mineral

igneous: rock formed by the crystallization of magma

intrusive: igneous rock that forms below the earth's surface

ion: atom that becomes positively or negatively charged because of the loss or gain of an electron

iridescence: visual rainbow effect caused by tiny crystals growing on a mineral

joint: natural break between layers of rock

labradorescence: schiller like the surface of a soap bubble

luminescence: emission of light

luster: the visual surface texture of a mineral

magma: molten rock under the earth's surface

metamorphic: rock formed by heat or pressure

opalescence: schiller containing all colors of the rainbow

opaque: not allowing light to pass through

ore: rock containing a mineral that can be profitably extracted

photoluminescence: emission of light from a mineral

piezoelectric: generating electricity when squeezed or bent

pigmentation: the natural color of a mineral, as shown by its streak

pleochroism: the ability of a crystal to absorb wavelengths of light differently, resulting in it showing distinct colors in different directions

pluton: gigantic mass of intrusive igneous rock that forms when magma solidifies

polymorphic: without a consistent shape

pyroelectric: generating electricity when heated

quencher: ion that prevents a mineral from being fluorescent

radioactivity: emission of alpha, beta, and gamma rays from uranium minerals

radioluminescence: emission of light from a mineral when irradiated

reflection: the visual effect when light hits a surface and bounces off of it

refraction: the bending of white light through a crystal, splitting it into a spectrum of colors

schiller: play of light on a mineral's surface, caused by combined reflection and refraction

sedimentary: rocks formed by deposition of eroded pieces of pre-existing rocks

sill: magma sheet flowing horizontally between layers of rock

skarn: metamorphic rock created by intrusion of gases

strata: layers of rock

streak: a line showing the color pigments in a mineral

syncline: a trough of stratified rock in which the layers bend upward in two directions from a base

thermoluminescence: emission of light from a mineral when heated

translucent: not clear, but allowing light to pass through

transparent: clear, able to be seen through

triboluminescence: emission of light from a mineral when rubbed or broken

trichromatic: showing pleochroism in three colors

vug : hollow in rock, caused by escaping gas or erosion

FURTHER READING

Barnes-Svarney, Patricia L. *Born of Heat and Pressure: Mountains and Metamorphic Rocks.* Springfield, NJ: Enslow, 1991.

Bates, Robert L. *Mineral Resources A–Z.* Springfield, NJ: Enslow, 1991.

Busbey, Arthur, Robert R. Coenraads, and David Roots. *Rocks & Fossils (Nature Company Guide).* Alexandria, VA: Time-Life Books, 1996.

Fuller, Sue. *Rocks & Minerals.* (A Pockets Book). New York: Dorling Kindersley, 1995.

Kerrod, Robin. *Mineral Resources.* New York: Thomson Learning, 1994.

Kittinger, Jo S. *A Look at Minerals: From Galena to Gold.* Danbury, CT: Franklin Watts, 1998.

Kittinger, Jo S. *A Look at Rocks: From Coal to Kimberlite.* Danbury, CT: Franklin Watts, 1997.

Lye, Keith. *Rocks, Minerals and Fossils.* Parsippany, NJ: Silver Burdett, 1991.

Pellant, Chris. *Collecting Gems & Minerals.* New York: Sterling, 1998.

Pellant, Chris, Harry Taylor, and Helen Pelland. *Eyewitness Handbooks: Rocks & Minerals.* New York: Dorling Kindersley, 1992.

Ricciuti, Edward R. *National Audubon Society First Field Guide: Rocks & Minerals.* New York: Scholastic: 1998.

Tilling, Robert I. *Born of Fire: Volcanoes and Igneous Rocks.* Springfield, NJ: Enslow, 1991.

Woodward, Christine, and Roger Harding. *Gemstones.* New York: Sterling, 1988.

ON THE WORLD WIDE WEB

Since the Internet is constantly changing, websites come and go. These are a few mineral-related websites that have been around for many years. To look for others, use a good search engine and try keywords like "rocks," "fossils," "minerals," "rockhounding," "mineralogy," and "mining."

Athena Mineralogy
http://un2sg4.unige.ch/athena/mineral/mineral.html
This large, searchable database of mineral information is presented by the Faculty of Science at the University of Geneva, Switzerland.

Bob's Rock Shop
http://www.rockhounds.com
A collection of images and information about minerals and how to collect them, this noncommercial site is hosted by Bob Keller, an avid mineral collector.

Chem4Kids
http://www.chem4kids.com
Learn the elemental information about the elements at this chemistry site just for kids, hosted by Rader New Media.

The Evolving Earth
http://www.150.si.edu/150trav/discover/evolve.htm
Part of the Smithsonian Museum of Natural History's Discovery Gallery, this website features information on earth science, rocks, and minerals.

Mineral Collection of École des Mines de Paris

http://cri.ensmp.fr/mineral/catalogue.html

This catalog of mineral images and information is from one of the world's finest mineralogical schools, the School of Mines in Paris, France.

Mineral Gallery

http://mineral.galleries.com/

A gigantic collection of photographs of minerals and mineralogical data is classified by physical characteristics, elements, and names. This educational website is hosted by Amethyst Galleries, Inc., a mineral dealer.

Minerals and Metals: A World to Discover

http://www.nrcan.gc.ca/mms/school/e_mine.htm

An educational tour about the mining and use of minerals and metals in everyday life; includes information on mineral-related careers. From Natural Resources Canada.

Smithsonian Gem & Mineral Collection

http://galaxy.einet.net/images/gems/gems-icons.html

Beautiful photos of highlights from the Smithsonian Museum of Natural History's gem and mineral collection.

PLACES TO VISIT

There are hundreds of excellent mineral collections in museums all over North America. Most natural history museums devote at least one hall to their mineral collection. **The Smithsonian Museum of Natural History** (Washington, D.C.) opened its new Janet Annenberg Hooker Hall of Geology, Gems and Minerals in 1997. It's huge: over eight football fields' worth of rocks and minerals, and there are plenty of computer workstations and hands-on exhibits to keep you busy for hours.

Other natural history museums with great mineral presentations include the **Royal Ontario Museum** in Ontario, Canada; the **Carnegie Museum of Natural History** in Pittsburgh, PA; the **Houston Museum of Natural History** in Houston, TX; the **Los Angeles Museum of**

Natural History in Los Angeles, CA; and the **American Museum of Natural History** in New York, NY. Specialty museums focusing on regional minerals include the **A.E. Seaman Museum**, deep in the heart of Michigan's copper country (Houghton, MI) and the **Missouri Mines State Historic Site** (Park Hills, MO) in the Tri-State lead-zinc mining district.

Underground tours are a fun way to learn about minerals and mining. At **Science North** in the mining town of Sudbury, Ontario (705-522-3701), you can watch movies in a theater carved in rock, swap minerals at the swap shop, walk underground through the Big Nickel Mine, and take a tour through the International Nickel Company's busy copper and nickel mining works. At the **Queen Mine** (Bisbee, AZ, 520-432-5421), you put on a hard hat and battery-powered lamp to explore one of the most productive copper mines in the United States.

Looking for a gold mine? At the **Timmins Underground Mine Tour** (Timmins, Ontario, 705-267-2222) you change into mining gear at the miners' change house, then walk down into a gold mine that first opened in 1909. At the **Old Hundred Gold Mine** (Silverton, CO, 800-872-3009), you ride a rail car 1,500 feet (457 meters) down into the mine. The **Sterling Hill Mining Museum** (Ogdensburg, NJ, 973-209-7212) offers a walk through the top level of a zinc mine, showing off fluorescent minerals underground and mining apparatus above. At **Soudan Underground Mine State Park** (Soudan, MN, 218-753-2245), you ride in the miner's elevator 2,341 feet (714 meters) into the earth, then board railroad cars to examine how miners extracted iron ore. The **Sierra Silver Mine Tour** (Wallace, ID, 208-752-5151) illustrates hard-rock silver mining.

Several tours take you into the dark world of coal mines: the **Lackawanna Coal Mine Tour** (Lackawanna, PA, 717-963-MINE), the **Tour-Ed Mine** (Tarentum, PA, 724-224-4720), the **Seldom Seen Coal Mine** (Patton, PA, 800-237-8590), and the **Beckley Exhibition Coal Mine** (Beckley, WV, 304-256-1747).

Finally, there are places where the whole family can collect minerals together. The **Franklin Mineral Museum** (Franklin, NJ, 973-827-3481) has the world's largest collection of fluorescent minerals, and you can collect some of your own on the Buckwheat Dump. The **Morefield**

Mine (Amelia, VA, 804-561-3399) lets you dig and pan for gemstones and their world-famous amazonite. Summertime in **Bancroft, Ontario**, means geologist-led field trips to the many old mines tucked away in the region's forests (613-332-1513). The **Ruggles Mine** (Grafton, NH, 603-523-4275) is a feldspar and mica mine with dozens of different minerals. At **Sheffler's Geode Mine** (Alexandria, MO, 816-754-6443) you can dig for geodes big and small. **Fairy Stone State Park** (Stuart, VA, 540-930-2424) is famous for its natural staurolite crosses that you can dig up and keep. **Crater of Diamonds State Park** (Murfeesboro, AR, 870-285-3113) lets you search for and take home diamonds. It's the only place in the United States where diamonds are found.

For information on many other museums and mines, and places where you can find excellent minerals on your own, consult magazines like *Rock & Gem*, *Rocks & Minerals*, *The Mineralogical Record*, *Mineral News*, and *Lapidary Journal*. These magazines often describe "field trips" to mineral-collecting sites across North America. The *Gem Guides* series of books (Gem Guides Publishing) is also a good place to find exact directions to well-known mineral-collecting sites.

INDEX